We A

My Extraterrestrial Contact

Kristi Pederson

"Always keep your mind open. In all things, always keep your mind open. Everything is possible. Especially things you know nothing about."

- Neale Donald Walsch

"If I become president, I'll make every piece of information this country has about UFO sightings available to the public and scientists. I am convinced that UFOs exist because I have seen one."
President Jimmy Carter

Acknowledgments

No book is written alone. It takes the input and help from many to make this a finished product worth reading.

I'd like to thank Dr. Jack Kasher, Angela Pennisi, and Gabriele Kohlieber for listening to my story without judgment.

Thank you to Marina Gray for your brutal edits – I love you, girl.

Thank you to the ET support group, which continues to educate and enlighten every day.

Thank you to the brave people who've gone before me with their stories of abduction. I couldn't have told my story without your courage.

Finally, thank you to the readers who understand that we are not alone and have never been alone.

Table of Contents

Foreward

Kristi has written an excellent and incisive summary of her life, and the growth and depth she has been drawn to. Each stage, from when she was a young child up to the present, has widened and deepened her spiritual development and awareness of who she is, and where she is headed.

Some of her experiences are beyond what most would consider normal, particularly those that deal with extraterrestrials and her development as a psychic. These might lead more conservative individuals to think that those experiences are too "far out" for them to relate to. But this is part of her life story and must be included in the whole picture.

I think the book is an important portrayal of her spiritual and psychic gifts, and her personal story should lead some to her for her contribution to their spiritual and psychic growth. I hope that many will be drawn to this book, leading them to an understanding of the many facets that have developed her into where she is right now. In addition, hopefully many will contact her, and profit from their personal mutual interaction.

Dr. Jack Kasher, Ph.D
Professor Emeritus of Physics
The University of Nebraska at Omaha

Introduction

Everyone has pieces of themselves that they keep hidden from the rest of the world. I was one of those people. Usually, the hidden pieces are those things we're not proud of or in which we fear judgment from others if exposed. In my case, it was both.

After a 2010 declaration to part of my family that I would heal no matter what it looked like, my healing journey began by working with childhood wounds. As I worked through family issues, I found my self-confidence growing and my fears diminishing. Courage showed its face. I was giving myself permission to be me.

One of my favorite Oscar Wilde quotes is, "Be yourself. Everyone else is already taken." This quote is humorous but profound, which makes it perfect. As I claimed myself step by step, I noticed less judgment from others and from myself towards others. Each year I uncovered a smidgeon more of who I was and who I wanted to be, but there always seemed to be a stopping point that, if revealed, would feel like I'd crossed the Rubicon or to the point of no return. I wasn't yet brave enough to go beyond that point.

I was a closeted psychic medium most of my life but had been subjected to enough judgment from others when uncensored things would fly out of my mouth. I learned early to keep quiet. It took three years of working with alternative healers to finally claim that part of myself. I knew it was okay to be a psychic medium and that it was a gift I could share with others. I was making progress but still not brave enough to reveal my biggest secret – that I was a contactee, a person who had alien abduction experiences.

Divulging this part of my life gave me pause. I watched the news and listened to reports about UFOs. The people who claimed to have seen a craft were always made to look absurd. For many years, I refused to set myself up to be ridiculed.

However, there comes a time in many people's lives where it just doesn't matter anymore; you must give up and retreat into yourself or you must be brave and stand up for yourself. For me, that time is now. There is more than my reputation and integrity at stake. What is at stake is the healing of other people who have had similar experiences but have no place to go, no one to talk to, and no one who will understand what they've been through. I am that person. I am here to help and to understand. Dr. Jack Kasher extended a hand to help me more than two decades ago, and now it's time to pay it forward.

Why Me?

Why me is the question I've asked myself for decades. Why was I chosen to be experimented on by extraterrestrials or space beings? Why was I chosen to be taken from my home during the night? Why was I being prepared for things of which I had no concept? Why was I exposed to phenomena that scared me to death but then left me with no one to talk to, no one to share these events with? If I did tell my friends and family, would they be judgmental just as I was judging myself? Was I crazy? Should I be committed to an institution? If I told anyone, would they – could they - have me committed?

Those were the questions constantly going through my mind as I began my journey of discovering who I was, why was I here, and why these extraordinary things were happening. You see, I've been an abductee of extraterrestrials for many years. Through my journey of healing and understanding, I now like to use the terms contactee or experiencer, sometimes even the word partner. They seem more palatable somehow.

I now have some answers to these questions and realize part of my journey is to share my ordeals with others going through the same terrifying experiences I've been through – am still going through - and help them understand their own journey and try to make sense of it all. By finally summoning the courage to tell my stories to a world who might not understand, I hope others feeling lost, alone, and distressed can begin their own healing. We can question together – IS the world ready to understand us? This is a chance I'm willing to take. I want the world to see the bigger picture of who we are, who we are becoming, and who we want to be, even if it means risking ridicule and judgment.

My life of 64 years consists of compartmentalized puzzle pieces that I've spent countless hours and thousands of dollars trying to put together in a way that I could comprehend, let alone share with others. Since much of my memory of interactions with space beings was downloaded in non-chronological order, I've found it difficult to communicate in a way that might make sense to you. Downloads feel like blocks of information received all at once rather than in the linear way most of us are accustomed to receiving information. Therefore, I've broken down my series of experiences in groupings, by chapter, to help you understand what can happen during an abduction, which causes trauma not only to the physical body but also mainly to the emotional body.

I am not an expert in ufology or abductions and can only speak from my own experiences. My downloads sometimes happened years after an event. Often, it felt like I hadn't been taken or contacted for months or even years when suddenly a download would happen and years' worth of experiments, abductions, and technological training would enter my brain, only to drop me to my knees with the terror and confusion of it all.

One day I was on my morning walk and feeling happy, upbeat, and ready to take on the world. During the walk I realized that I hadn't been taken by space beings in what felt like some time. No sooner had the thought entered my mind than downloads happened. I had not only been abducted regularly, but I had also been taken as recently as the night before. My legs went weak, and I crawled to a nearby bench on the trail. I sat there, tears streaming down my face, for more than half an hour until I could wrap my head around what had just happened.

With every other abduction up to that point, I felt numb and confused when the downloads happened and memory kicked in. This download was different. My walk began with a feeling of joy and carefree abandon but was interrupted with a download so strong it took my breath away. The download informed me that the abductions were still happening, and the attitude with which the download was delivered had the energy of predators with their prisoner. There was no escape. They had control, and I was at their mercy.

What affected me the most was not only the abductions themselves but also the fact that the aliens could download information, at will, into my head. They could manipulate me in almost any way they chose. By downloading or withholding information, these space beings made me question what was real versus what they wanted me to see.

The memories I've chosen to share are coming from what I've been able to cobble together through decades of contact with space beings, experts in the field of ufology, hypnosis, and many other methods of alternative healing. I'm also a psychic medium, which figures into my recall of abduction events. I've often asked myself if my experiences with space beings contributed to my psychic abilities or if I was selected by space beings because of my psychic abilities. Being a psychic medium has helped me remember many abductions, medical experiments, flying crafts, and introductions to my own hybrid children. My psychic abilities have also bestowed upon me a gift for listening and healing. As you'll discover, not all the contact was bad, often making it more difficult to wrap my head around what was happening to me. Most abductions were physically invasive, but many were educational. I experienced abductions by two different groups of space beings. Most abductions consisted of physically invasive examinations by a group of beings that included doctors and helpers. I also was abducted by a group of beings who taught me advanced technological programming

In my research, I've had the opportunity to communicate with ufologist and filmmaker Linda Moulton Howe, American historian and alien abduction author Dr. David Jacobs, UFO educator and hypnotist Denise Stoner, and professor of physics and astronomy at UNO (University of Nebraska) and UFO researcher Dr. Jack Kasher. But let's start at the beginning of my story. My first memory of feeling different and knowing that something odd was happening began at the age of five. It took 25 years to figure out I was in contact with space beings. It took decades after that to make sense of it all.

*"Yes, there have been crashed craft, and bodies recovered.
We are not alone in the universe;
They have been coming here for a long time."*
Edgar Mitchell, NASA Astronaut, Apollo 14

NDE

At the age of five, I had a near-death experience or what is known as an NDE. It wasn't the NDE you typically read about. There wasn't an accident; I didn't leave my body, meet God, and then get sent home. However, I was sick. Very sick. I was dehydrated and couldn't stop throwing up from a case of the flu that just wouldn't end. On day five of me being sick, my mother, who was 28 years old at the time, was frazzled beyond belief. Everyone in the family had had this flu, including my dad, my eight-year-old older sister, and my twin sister. But I was the only one who couldn't seem to kick it. This was 1960 when we, like most families, owned only one car. My father drove it to and from work each day, so my mother couldn't just bundle me up and rush to the hospital.

My mother did the best she could with what was available. I remember her propping me upside down on the sofa so I wouldn't choke on my own vomit. She put a bucket on the floor right under my face to make it easier for me to not make a mess. I didn't know which was more important, my comfort or a clean house. This may sound harsh, but that was my mother, ever practical.

By today's standards, how my mother treated me during my illness sounds like cruel and unusual punishment. However, in 1960 it seemed like the logical thing to do. After five days, my mother finally called the doctor, Dr. Edith Burns, who told my mother to take me to Sioux Valley hospital immediately and she would meet us there. Then mom called dad at work, and he rushed home to stay with my sisters so mom could take me to the hospital.

I was admitted to the hospital that afternoon. Back then, parents could not stay after a certain time of night. So, as difficult as this is to believe now, my mother left me with a raging fever in the care of doctors and nurses she trusted to make me well.

During the night I remember being put in an ice bed, which was a hospital bed, jury-rigged with a sheet tied to the four corners of the bed frame. It created a "V" in the center of the bed that was then filled with ice and covered with a blanket. I was placed on top of the blanket while a nurse stood at the head of the bed and force-fed me cold orange soda to hopefully bring down my temperature. The cool blanket felt soothing against my hot skin but did little to lower my fever.

The nurse, I remember, was young, pretty, and so kind. I could feel her concern and care as she wiped perspiration from my forehead with a cold cloth. She kept trying to keep me awake by telling me how much I liked orange soda. She was right; I did love orange soda, but tonight all I wanted was to sleep and drift off to someplace quiet. Being awakened every five minutes felt so rude. I just wanted to go home, but the place I was yearning for wasn't the home where I lived just a few miles away. It was someplace else, someplace I'd never visited but knew existed.

During a break of drinking soda, which was beginning to taste sickeningly sweet and sticky, I remember the nurse standing still, as if she was paralyzed. Her eyes looked glazed over, and her smile was frozen on her face. I was suddenly wide awake and looked around, wondering what was wrong with her. Why wasn't she trying to wake me up like she'd been doing the entire night? Why was she not talking, not moving? Although I was awake, I still couldn't lift my head. All I could do was move my eyes to see above me where the nurse stood and on either side of me. Those minor movements were enough for me to know something wasn't as it should be. My room was suddenly quiet too; my breathing was the only sound. There were no machines running, no one in the hall talking, and no outside ambient noise of any kind.

Around that time, someone, who appeared to be a doctor, entered my room. He wore a white medical jacket and had a stethoscope hanging out of the lower jacket pocket. What was so weird, even to a five-year-old, was that the stethoscope reflected a blinding, bright light obscuring his face. What was it reflecting off? There was no light in my room. The light was so glaringly bright that it diffused the face of the doctor to the point that I couldn't make it out at all.

Even though I couldn't see his face, he still didn't look like any doctor I'd ever seen. There was something about his energy that somehow just didn't seem right or normal. He positioned himself on the right side of the bed next to me and leaned over my bed. As he did so, I remember him communicating telepathically. I certainly didn't know what telepathy was at age five. All I knew was that he made no noise and didn't even move his lips, but I understood everything he was communicating. He told me not to worry and that I would always be safe and protected. I remember thinking, of course I'm safe and protected. Why wouldn't I be? After all, I was a little girl with a loving family, so nothing was a threat at that time. I don't know how long he was there; but when he left, the nurse moved again and asked me to drink more orange soda, which I then swore I would never drink again. We picked up where we'd left off: me wanting to sleep and her force-feeding me the now despised orange soda. Years later, under hypnosis, I discovered that the being I saw as a doctor wasn't the only one who entered my room that night, and none were human.

The next day my parents came to visit me at the hospital and were told by the doctor, "We almost lost her last night." Neither I nor my parents knew how sick I really was. I felt no physical pain, which was the only determining way my parents and I judged being sick. I was blissfully unaware of what I was going through, only that I wanted to be left alone to go somewhere else. Although I vividly remember being so sick and, in the hospital, I had no way of knowing I nearly died that night until my mother told me over 40 years later. Perhaps my visit by this strange doctor was a hallucination, and on one level, I can't disagree. On another level, however, this event of my childhood has shown up often in hypnotherapy. As I've tried to put the puzzle pieces of my life together the pieces of my life that shape my story start, as they do for most humans, with my family.

Family Life

I know many people blame their parents and the rest of their family for their troubles in life. I've always believed that when we come into this human existence, we choose our parents and our siblings. So really, there is no one to blame but ourselves. We choose these other spirits, masquerading as family members, to help us learn the lessons we are here to learn. But again, I asked myself the question, why? Why did I pick these particular people to help me on my path? As much as I tried to fit in with my family, I was so different from them all; and having a twin sister just added an extra twist to the mix. It felt like a constant never-ending battle in the attempt to just be myself.

My sister and I were born in the mid-1950s. Back then twins were expected to look, dress, and BE alike. My twin and I couldn't have been more different. I was an extrovert to her introvert; and while she was a homebody, I thought about what the rest of the world was like outside of our small town in South Dakota. Since we were fraternal twins, biologically, we weren't more similar than any other siblings, but twins being different was not the accepted way of the fifties.

My sisters, younger brother, who was born in 1961, and I liked to watch Saturday morning cartoons like most kids did. We all liked Looney Tunes, Popeye, and other popular shows of the day, but my favorite cartoon was The Jetsons. The Jetsons, a futuristic family of four and their dog, lived in space, somewhere in the distant future. Watching George Jetson, the father, fly his spaceship to work thrilled me. Spaceships somehow seemed much more normal than our stupid light blue Plymouth station wagon, which bumped along at an achingly slow speed. The Jetsons lived in Orbit City, and their apartment in the sky seemed exotic. They didn't have rotary dial phones like my family used. Instead, they would press a button and see each other over the phone! The Jetsons had Skype long before video conferencing had entered the public consciousness.

However, as visionary as the show was, the wife and mother, Jane Jetson, projected a very traditional persona. She wore curlers in her hair, put on too much make-up, and felt she had to look perfect to talk on the phone. If Jane received a phone call in the morning when she wasn't properly ready for the day, she put on a plastic face, which looked and moved exactly like her own face. She could have her video phone conversation and look like she was dressed to go out on the town. Okay, not everything in that show was space age; much of it mirrored the stereotypical male and female roles of the time. Nevertheless, my mind was opened to the possibilities of space travel and living in space, which seemed exciting but somehow very natural.

All four of the kids in my family were expected to have manners, behave impeccably, and act civilized, as were most children in the families with whom we were acquainted. My siblings seemed to get most things right, while I failed miserably most of the time. Many of the family rules of social etiquette just didn't make sense. Why couldn't I drink beer at a family outing? My parents rarely, if ever, drank alcohol; but occasionally, one of their friends might bring a beer to our house when we'd all sit outside during the hot summer months. Central air conditioning didn't exist; and only wealthier families had a window air conditioner, so the occasional beer for the adults was a treat to cool off. I'd never had a beer in my life but somehow it seemed appropriate at one 4th of July outing. After lunch, my parents and some of their friends were drinking hot coffee, which was the standard drink for them. However, I never understood why someone would drink hot coffee outside during a hot and humid day. Jokingly, one adult asked me if I would like a cup of coffee too. I looked her straight in the eye and at the age of five said, "Joan, little girls don't drink coffee!" She then said with mocking disdain in her voice, "Oh really? Well then, what do they drink?" I firmly shouted back to her, "Beer!" and then had a hissy fit when they wouldn't give me a beer. They finally surrendered and gave a sip to both my sister and me.

I made the frequent mortal sin of asking questions and challenging my parents, but instead of explaining things or letting me be me – different from my siblings – I was punished, sometimes humiliatingly so. I understood my parents were exasperated and not sure how to handle me. When even punishment didn't work, they eventually tried a psychologist. I was about 14 years old in the late 60s, and psychology was still very stigmatized then. Seeing a psychologist was considered a last resort, almost a failure on my parent's part in not knowing how to control my behavior. My mom's goal in taking me to a psychologist was to discover what was wrong with me. The psychologist who I only remember as being young and handsome even to a young teenager, asked me questions, and I answered in my usual way, with straight forward honesty and no diplomacy. He knew I was odd and different but not crazy or in need of psychological help. He challenged my mother about her parenting style, which meant we never went back, and things only went from bad to worse. At point in my life, the abductions happened, but I didn't receive the downloads of information and memory until I was in my 30s. As an adolescent, I just felt confused and fearful, which often exhibited itself as erratic, inappropriate behavior.

Earlier in my teens, I was experiencing physical symptoms too: frequent bloody noses and unrelenting motion sickness every time I would ride in a car or boat. No one else in my family physically faced anything remotely like what I was going through. I would wake up in the morning as usual, go to the kitchen to eat my breakfast of cold cereal and milk, and then blood would gush out of my nose. I wasn't in pain and couldn't even feel the blood running down my face until someone pointed it out to me or the metallic taste of blood would blend with the sweetness of my cereal. I'm not sure how often these nosebleeds would happen, but when they did occur, it felt like they would never stop. My mother would position me on the sofa with my head tilted back and put a homemade ice pack on my nose. Eventually, the nosebleed would stop, and I could continue my day. The frequency of these nosebleeds was alarming to my parents, so we were off to the family doctor once again. Our doctor concluded, without investing too much, that I was picking my nose too hard and causing the nosebleeds. I wasn't.

Later, hypnosis verified that the nosebleeds were caused by extraterrestrials inserting implants in my nasal passages. These implants are like minicomputer chips and are used in much the same way as the tracking devices scientists use on endangered species to record their movements and behavior in their natural habitat. The animal tags are electronically designed to locate the studied species and record important data. Implants from aliens, from my understanding and research, do much of the same things.

As for the motion sickness, my parents brought an empty coffee can and a washcloth on every car or boat ride to be used for the inevitable. No one else in my family EVER threw up from motion sickness – only me and on every trip. We'd be driving along as I felt the symptoms of nausea begin. The symptoms would start with saliva building up in my mouth and then the churning in my stomach, until both hot and cold sweat poured out of me. My lips would turn blue as a white line circled my mouth. I knew what was coming but held off telling my parents, hoping this time would be different. As saliva continued to build and the pouring sweat persisted, I couldn't hold it any longer as I would whisper, "Daddy, I have to spit." No one would even turn around to look. My father would slam on the brakes and pull over to the side of the road. My mom would grab the coffee can and wash cloth, jump out of the passenger seat, and open the car door to the back seat, as I tumbled out and threw up in the coffee can or beside the road, whichever was closest. When I was finished being sick, we'd all pile back in the car and off we'd go.

Hypnosis also clarified that this kind of motion sickness is very common in abductees. Being transported, or rather teleported, from Earth to a craft, which vibrates at a very different rate, can create many kinds of disturbances in equilibrium.

By the age of 12, I was old enough to start babysitting and earn some spending money in addition to the $.50 weekly allowance I received. The family I babysat for most weekends had four kids, including a newborn baby, and lived just cattycorner from the back of our house. Most babysitting sessions lasted for several hours, and often the parents wouldn't get home until two o'clock in the morning, sometimes even later. When the parents did get home, the mother would stand at their door and watch to make sure I made it home safely. When I left their house, I had to cross the street, climb a fence, fight my way through the dozens of lilac bushes surrounding our property, and in the spring, trample through a garden of peonies before I found grass and the path to my own back door. In today's world, that would never fly, but back in the 60s, watching children go home rather than escorting them was a convenient and standard practice.

Most nights, or rather early mornings, I would run out the door and race home, eager to find my own bed. On several occasions, however, I would make it over the fence and past the gardens only to lie down in the grass and stare at the stars in the sky. I was tempted to just stay there all night because the stars were beckoning me to my real home. I knew I couldn't stay long since I was being watched by the neighbor, but I took advantage of the time allowed and dreamed of a better place.

Every time this happened, the neighbor would call my mom the next day to tell her what happened, and of course, I would get in trouble. Just get home! Don't dawdle! What no one understood was that lying on the grass in the middle of the night was where I belonged. I belonged to the stars and the night sky and whatever else was out there waiting for me. Staring at a sky teeming with stars never frightened me. My fear was triggered by more earthly and mundane things, like the airport metal detector.

My father, who was a purchasing agent for a local company in Sioux Falls, rarely traveled for business. However, when he did, the sendoff became a family adventure, and we'd all trek out to the airport to give dad a proper goodbye. When I was 15, hijacking events happened more frequently and received national coverage on the evening news. Security measures were put into place at airports around the country. On one farewell for my father, I saw the first metal detector installed in the Sioux Falls airport. To me, the metal detector looked like an open door leading to nowhere. Its purpose was to beep when any guns were being brought on board the airplane, and therefore, eliminate possible future hijackings. When I first saw the metal detector, a white plastic and metal doorframe about three feet thick, I knew I was expected to walk through in order to escort my dad to his gate.

I couldn't do it. I could not walk through that doorway no matter what explanations or threats were imposed on me. My parents were furious, yelling at me that I was immature and stubborn and asking why I couldn't do something so simple. At one point, to placate me, my mother even offered to hold my hand and walk through that door to nowhere with me. I flatly refused and said that I'd sit on a bench in the ticketing area and wait for my dad's plane to leave and for the rest of the family to return. For a reason I couldn't explain, I was scared to death. I had the feeling that if I walked through that doorway, something horrible would happen to me. What that horrible thing might be, I didn't know. But the fear was palpable, and the nausea in my stomach was threatening to erupt.

Years later, under hypnosis, it became very clear that my fear was a result of being taken aboard different UFO crafts and walking through very similar doorways to examining rooms where I would be subjected to experiments and violated in every way imaginable and unimaginable. Things were totally out of my control during an abduction when I was on a craft; but now, in the middle of an airport, I was not going to let that happen, not when I could exercise some control. I never did go through that doorway. My parents finally gave up and let me sit on a bench outside of security. Unconsciously, I was scared to death when triggered by certain unexplainable items or events. I was so confused, defiant, and petrified often, all at the same time.

My odd behavior continued throughout my teenage years. On weekends when I didn't have to be up early for school, I would sleep until noon and then sit on our screened in front porch until two o'clock in the morning, just contemplating life and the night sky. The more my confusion increased, the more misunderstood I felt; and I became more and more of an anomaly to my family. To escape myself and my family, I began using drugs, mostly marijuana at the time. The use of pot made me begin to question everything I'd been taught, especially my religious upbringing. My questions were philosophical in nature, such as if God is all loving, why are we supposed to fear him? Or if someone commits a sin and is sentenced to hell, and the church decided that sin wasn't a sin anymore, where do they go? Heaven? Or are they still stuck in hell forever? I wasn't satisfied with the answers from my parents or from the local youth minister at the Lutheran church we attended, which is why, at my high school graduation party at the age of 17, I announced that I was an atheist. I'd never heard the word agnostic – questioning the existence of God – so I used a word I did know: atheist.

Right after graduation, my parents told me I had to start paying rent or move out. I found a small apartment within a couple of weeks, and for the first time, lived on my own.

Married Life

I loved the independence of living away from my parent's home; and even though it was just two miles away, it felt like another town completely. My rent in my new basement apartment was $40 a month. I didn't own a car, so expenses were minimal. I walked or rode my bike everywhere. When I pedaled to the grocery store, I could only purchase one bag of groceries at a time. I didn't have a basket on my bike, so I held the paper bag of groceries with one arm and steered my bike with the other. I couldn't have been happier doing the simplest things. The independence of paying rent, buying groceries, doing laundry, and especially buying my own clothes in the latest fashion was a freedom I drank up like ice cold lemonade on a hot summer day.

I created my own life free of the constraints of my family. I didn't have to fit in with anybody; I could finally just be me. That trip of self-discovery didn't last long. On one hand, I wanted freedom and the peace it brought. But I was so used to turmoil, criticism, and not fitting in because I had a deep need to re-create what I was accustomed to in my twisted little comfort zone. I hated the chaos and yet chased it relentlessly. I had no idea what peace and balance looked or felt like, so I fell back to what I knew – creating confusion, drama, and trouble. At 19, I thought the perfect solution was to get married.

In my mind I thought that if I got married, my husband would take care of me, love me unconditionally, and my life would finally be perfect. My parents would finally accept me because, with a husband, I would fit their expectations of what my life should be. My future husband and I met on a blind date on December 21st, 1973. Six months later, we were engaged; and exactly one year from our first date, we were married.

It worked for a while, at least during the engagement and planning of the wedding. My parents loved my fiancé. He fit their mold perfectly by being tall, dark, handsome, a soon-to-be college graduate, and on the fast track to a career in journalism. He was every parent's dream for their daughter; so my parents embraced him, the wedding, and me. My mom and I became close for the first time since I could remember. I'm sure my mother thought my husband would be the answer to fixing all that was wrong with me. My tastes in designing a wedding differed greatly from what she would have chosen, but she went along with my choices, delirious that I was going to finally settle down and live a normal life, or her idea of a normal life.

A few weeks before the wedding, I started having doubts. Was he what I wanted in a husband, a life partner? I saw the differences in us rather than the similarities that would enable us to build a beautiful life together. One day I was looking to the heavens, and I asked if I was doing the right thing. I distinctly heard a voice reply to my question. The voice told me to marry this man as his proposal would be the only one I would ever receive in this lifetime. Years later it became very clear that I was to marry this man, especially if it didn't last. This may sound confusing, but I was told by the voice, which I now know was one of my spirit guides, that I was to marry for a short amount of time and then divorce. I was to get the romance thing out of my system by realizing that marriage was not for me. My life was meant to focus on a metaphysical journey and not waste time yearning for "the one" like most young people do. My life was meant for other things.

On my wedding day, I clearly recall walking down the aisle to marry the man I loved and feeling blissfully happy. After the minister pronounced us man and wife, we walked back down the aisle to clapping and cheering. During that brief walk, however, I heard in my head a different voice, which I now know was an additional spirit guide, asking me what the hell I'd just done. The twisting of doubt and restlessness in the pit of my stomach had resurfaced and would only get worse.

One day in our first year of marriage, I remember sitting at the dining room table crying. My husband came home and asked me what was wrong. I'd just brought in the mail and every envelope was labeled Mr. and Mrs. "His Name." I looked at the envelope and realized the only thing that represented me in the address was the S in Mrs. Everything else belonged to him. I felt insignificant and like I didn't matter. This was now 1974, and equality in marriage had not yet made its way to South Dakota.

Living together before marriage was still considered relatively taboo. However, before we were married, we did live together in Brookings, South Dakota where we both attended college. Since Brookings was 45 miles away from Sioux Falls, we were able live together secretly with neither of our parents knowing. I kept a dorm room as cover in case any of my family came to visit, and I could pretend that I lived there. Our home together was on the outskirts of this small college town where the dirt and gravel roads only led to wheat, corn fields, and little else. Those dirt roads were my salvation and the next painful step in my journey to me.

Before I convinced myself to be happy on my wedding day, I was already feeling signs of being miserable in this relationship. At night, I walked the dirt road just like my 12-year-old younger self, looked up at the stars, and asked to be taken home. I didn't belong in this relationship, in this life, or even on this planet. I shook my fist at the sky and yelled that I'd bitten off more than I could chew by taking on these challenges. I needed help, please! The biggest challenge was just living – surviving. It took every ounce of courage I could muster to get through each day. On the outside, I had friends and two jobs and was going to school. I appeared to have my life together and was on the perfect mainstream path I knew society expected of me. On the inside, I was desperate. It felt like being an artist in a world where art doesn't exist. What do you do? How do you fit in? How do you express yourself? You just muddle through and wonder why you don't fit in. That's what I did. I muddled, I stumbled, and then I berated myself for not being happy and not knowing what to do next. After my husband graduated from college and I dropped out, we moved back to Sioux Falls so he could begin his career and I could emotionally support him in the way I thought he needed. We both worked full time, but I thought I was a failure as a wife if there wasn't a home cooked meal on the table every night. By home cooked, I mean homemade bread, meat, potatoes, vegetable and a homemade dessert. Absolutely nothing came out of a box. I was exhausted, and he appreciated none of the time or effort it took to cook, which led to arguments and more discontent. During one fight he clearly expressed that he never once asked for elaborate meals. Instead of that declaration making me feel relieved, I felt worse than ever. I was claiming my worth through cooking and baking. For my husband to say he didn't want or even like these meals felt like he didn't want or like me either.

The expression I said to anyone who would listen back then was, "I made my bed, so now I have to lie in it." It felt like a brave and right thing to say. What I wanted to yell to the world was that I'd made a mistake. I told that last part only to myself, imposing a life sentence of living in an unhappy marriage. I claimed the life of a martyr and wore that badge of burden well.

Around this time, I met a friend through work. She was the proverbial wild child, and I admired almost everything about her. She didn't care what anybody thought about her or the things she did. She partied fast and hard, and she wanted company. I was the perfect person and happily volunteered to accompany her on the road to self-destruction. I'd never been much of a drinker, but she drank enough for the both of us as we went out together to the local hot spots. The more I partied, the more I hated my husband. The more I partied, the more frustrated he became. I asked him to go to counseling together, but he flatly refused. Every time he refused, I added one more night of partying to the weekly calendar. I tricked myself into thinking I was finally claiming who I was. I was angry and resentful and sought people who seemed confident and free. Never brave enough to lead, I let myself become a follower of people I thought I admired. I never considered whether they cared about my wellbeing. I was looking to escape, and my new friends provided the path.

This went on for about two years until a simple event put me on a path that changed my life forever.

"The Mars Rover currently has sent back images of some odd things on the surface of Mars, and some people think they could be UFOs. Here's my question, If we're on the surface of Mars, aren't we the UFOs?"
Jay Leno, The Tonight Show, 2012

Introduction to Metaphysics

My journey into the world of metaphysics, the study of abstract concepts, began by reading one simple book. When people have major changes in their lives, they usually remember the exact moment it happened. Although I don't remember the exact date, I recall the exact situation when my life changed. I was 21 years old, living in Sioux Falls and unhappily married.

My twin sister and I spoke often, and one day she phoned to tell me about a book she'd just finished called *The Search for Bridey Murphy*. She went on to explain that this book made her believe in reincarnation and shifted her perception of what dying meant. My attitude towards anyone and everyone at this time was hurtful and grandiose. I could hardly wait to get off the phone, go to the library, and borrow the book. I intended to read the book cover to cover, point out all the glaring errors, and prove to my sister how stupid the book was and how gullible she was.

Within 24 hours I'd gone to the library and had the book in my possession. As I read, not only could I not find any glaring errors, I was mesmerized. This was back in 1976, and metaphysical books were few, especially in Sioux Falls, South Dakota. *The Search for Bridey Murphy* was written about Virginia Tighe, a Colorado housewife undergoing hypnotic regression. Her hypnotist, Morey Bernstein, attempted to take her further back in her childhood than they'd gone in previous hypnosis sessions. Virginia surprised Morey by going one step further than childhood. She went back to the life of a 19th-century Irish woman named Bridey Murphy. Virginia, with a strong Irish accent, told of her life in Cork, Ireland. During subsequent sessions, Virginia would continue the saga of her previous life as Bridey Murphy.

Since its publication in 1956, there has been much research done on *The Search for Bridey Murphy;* and, therefore, controversy has followed. But in 1976 this was my first exposure to anything metaphysical, and I was hooked. Not only did I not chastise my sister about this book, I thanked her for mentioning it and frequented the local library to see what else was out there written about the metaphysical world.

Other books I discovered were *The Search for the Girl with the Blue Eyes* and *Edgar Cayce: The Sleeping Prophet*, both by Jess Stearn. *The Search for the Girl with the Blue Eyes* is similar to *The Search for Bridey Murphy* in which a teenage girl, Joanne MacIver, recalls a past life as a farmer's wife in Canada. *The Sleeping Prophet* is a biography about the life of Edgar Cayce, a photographer, who would go into a trans-like sleep to diagnose illnesses and subsequent cures. His books are still revered today. He is known as the father of holistic medicine and even built a Metaphysical center in Virginia Beach called A.R.E., or the Association for Research and Enlightenment.

These books were my teachers, guides, and mentors. As I read and studied anything I could get my hands on, I felt like I was finding me or at least an explanation for why I was the way I was. With every book I read, my life began to make sense. I gained an internal understanding of who we are as a species and why we're here.

Unfortunately, my new studies had the opposite effect on my friends and family who weren't ready to hear about any of that woo-woo stuff. I was becoming even more difficult to understand. Although I internalized the material I was reading, I had yet to assimilate it into my behavior. My husband and I saw no solution to our growing problems, which included my shifting beliefs; so we separated.

During the separation, my wild friend and I cranked up our party lives into high gear. We were out in the bars every single night. When the bars closed, we found friendly strangers to continue the party at some run-down house or apartment. My drug use escalated. I gave up pot, started to enjoy cocaine, speed, Quaaludes, and mushrooms. Why was I compelled to live like this? What was I running from? What was I running towards? Why couldn't I be happy and content with life as it was? Why did I always have to have drama in my life? Once again, on my own, why couldn't I be happy? I acted like I was happy, but happy people don't walk the road of self-destruction, do they?

One night, my friend and I left some stranger's house at about three in the morning and tried to find our way back to our own homes. We were so messed up, we didn't know which way was north, south, east, or west. We stopped on a bridge to gather our wits and figure out how to get home, when I heard a voice I didn't recognize, echoing in my brain and asking me in a very gentle way, "Is this really how you want to live your life?" Inside my head, feeling ashamed, I whispered back, "No! I don't."

I was in such a party routine; I didn't know how to separate myself from my friend and this life I'd created and the life I wanted to live. I was a skilled follower. I couldn't take the lead and announce I didn't want to do this anymore. So, I continued my late-night carousing, though the seed had been planted in my head that I needed to make changes. The problem was I didn't know where to begin, but I knew that South Dakota wasn't big enough for my now ex-husband and me. Just as I had moved out of my parents' house when I was 17, I believed another move might bring about the change I was seeking.

At 22 and before the ink was dry on my divorce papers, I packed my car with everything I owned and drove. I later told people I drove until I ran out of land and ended up in the bay area of California. I was so eager to begin a new life – again – that I received four speeding tickets on my way to California: one each in South Dakota, Wyoming, Montana, and Idaho. Yes, I was eager to make things different this time and live the perfect life. What I had yet to realize was that the change I needed to make was inside me and would not necessarily be achieved by changing friends, homes, or even states.

The day I arrived in San Mateo I found a job as a make-up artist at a local Merle Norman cosmetic studio and then connected with a friend of a friend, who agreed to let me live with her until I could get on my feet. That first night of my new life, my new friend took me to the best bar in San Mateo. She also introduced me to her drug dealer so I could have as much cocaine as my spartan budget could afford.

It seemed nothing had changed, except now I had an ocean nearby. As I sniffed the white powder laid out in lines in front of me, I flashed back to the five-year-old girl who was told that she would always be safe and protected. I knew I was still protected from the evils of the world, but I didn't know that I was safe from everyone but myself. I used to hear stories about people who would have an epiphany in their lives, and they would change dramatically and overnight. They would suddenly become these stellar humans and right their wrongs. I was not one of those people. I had an epiphany when I read *The Search for Bridey Murphy* and another one that night on the bridge in South Dakota, but my transformation to a better me happened so slowly that you couldn't tell any difference from day to day or month to month. But I WAS changing. I continued to study metaphysics and the paranormal, although ufology had yet to enter my consciousness. I studied and read every book I could find, even though I still had no one with whom I could discuss these things. Outside I was the same; but inside, little by little, seeds of change that had been planted were being watered and fertilized by reading, studying, and endless quests for more knowledge.

As I began to slowly wean myself away from the bad influences in my life, I landed a new job at a very upscale department store in San Mateo and made a new friend. She was a force to be reckoned with. Everyone loved her fierceness, boldness, and humor; and, for some reason, she took a liking to me. We became best friends from my first day on the job and, over forty years later, are still in contact with each other. She was my first positive influence, and I loved her for it. We worked together during the day and ate a dinner of popcorn at her home every night until it was time to go to bed. But when I left her house around nine or ten o'clock to go to my own home, I'd call upon the old crowd and out we'd go. Drugs and alcohol were still my nighttime friends, but between these very different lives, I read. And I kept on reading – reading and running. I was running from the truth of who I was, what was happening, and who I wanted to be.

As I became more serious about my career and taking better care of myself, I was offered a job with a major cosmetics company as a traveling make-up artist. I was the featured make-up artist in various stores from Carmel up to the Oregon border of California. I loved this job, the company, and the people I worked with; and for the first time, I was recognized for my contributions and commitment. A few years after moving to San Mateo, I was offered a promotion and transferred to Phoenix, Arizona. I lived there only two months when they promoted and transferred me again, this time to Knoxville, Tennessee. With each move

I became more and more corporate and less and less creative. My work ethic couldn't be challenged, and I didn't do drugs at all anymore. I'd also transitioned from being a make-up artist into the sales side of the cosmetic business. It meant more money, and finally, I was on my way, I thought. I was about to learn that I couldn't run or hide from myself. Wherever I went, there I was.

I've learned the universe has a funny way of helping you discover your life path and determination to get there. Just when things were looking up and I was living what I had always pictured as a successful life, a new boss was thrown in my path. He and I didn't see eye to eye on most things; and in a fit of anger at a company outing, I submitted my resignation, handwritten on a scrap piece of paper. Within two weeks I was on my way back to South Dakota where the wild friend was waiting. We picked up like no time had passed and were back to our old tricks, but my heart wasn't in it. I worked an assortment of low paying jobs and was just eking by financially and emotionally.

I relocated to Los Angeles for a dream job, but unfortunately, it didn't work out and only lasted a month. I then headed back to the Great Plains and ended up in Omaha, Nebraska, where I had a friend waiting for me. The minute she opened the door for me, I stood on her front porch and announced that I needed a job. After she invited me in, she mentioned that she'd met a guy in a bar about a year ago and she'd written his phone number on a bar napkin. If I could give her a few minutes she'd go to her basement and try to find it. I thought she was nuts but humored her. A few short minutes later she came up from the basement holding a wrinkled white bar napkin with a phone number written in black ink. I just laughed and thought I had nothing to lose by dialing the number. This was before caller ID, so I knew I could just hang up if needed and no one would be the wiser. After dialing the number someone answered, "Employment Agency." The guy she'd met in a bar a year ago worked for an employment agency?! I made an appointment for a few days later to meet with one of the consultants. The first question they asked was what I wanted to do. I answered that I didn't know. I had no clue. The consultant asked me if I was interested in becoming a buyer. I couldn't believe he was asking me if I wanted a dream job. Endless shopping with someone else's money? Where do I sign up?! After tests and interviews, I landed a respectable job as a merchandising assistant for a local department store chain, and within a year, was promoted to buyer.

This was a relatively new and growing company in which new employees were brought on board every month. Several of us newbies hit it off and immediately socialized together, which in my world meant drugs. Although I didn't partake of drugs like I used to, they were still around until one night when a flash of insight entered my consciousness. I noticed that I didn't even like some of the people I was with unless I was high. The next time we got together, I didn't like them even when I was sober. That night it was as if an internal light switch had been turned on. I never touched a drug again and never even had the desire. If anything, the opposite was true. I recoiled thinking about putting that kind of substance in my body. Finally, I knew drugs would never be a problem for me again.

Shortly after I gave up drugs, my psychic abilities started to kick into gear. Amazing what a clear head will allow to happen. I knew the psychic abilities had always been with me, but I chose to either not acknowledge them or just ignore them completely. By this time in my life, I'd already had enough psychic experiences to know and recognize the familiar eye roll from people who couldn't handle what was coming out of my mouth. When you are psychic, things can come out of your mouth sounding arrogant like a big know it all. That was never the intent; I just hadn't yet learned how to control or sensor the messages I was getting. Some people would physically step back to create distance between us. I learned quickly to bite my tongue and be careful with whom I shared my abilities. I became very good at keeping secrets: secrets I psychically knew about others and the secret of keeping my psychic gifts to myself. But the biggest secret I eventually had to learn to keep was just around the corner, waiting to introduce itself. It was waiting like a thief in the night, waiting to expose me to things I'd never even heard of, let alone had any experience with.

"It's my conclusion that UFOs do exist, are very real, and are spaceships from another or more than one solar system. They are possibly manned by intelligent observers who are members of a race carrying out long-range scientific investigations of our Earth for centuries."
Dr. Hermann Oberth, Father of Modern Space Travel

First Contact

I was 29 when I moved to Omaha, Nebraska. For ten years, I'd told my family and friends I didn't want to have children. Most people were surprised to hear this but understanding, except for my older sister. She kept telling me to wait until I was 30 to do anything about it since that's when my maternal instincts would kick in and I'd change my mind with no regrets. I took her advice and waited impatiently to turn 30. My 30th birthday present to myself was to have a tubal ligation so pregnancy would no longer be an option for me.

When I was younger, I assumed I would have children just like everybody else I knew. Somewhere along the way, that thought process changed, albeit gradually. It was getting so bad that when friends would tell me they were pregnant, my first emotion was shock. A look of horror would cross my face, and I would express sympathy and ask what they would do about it. My friends looked at me like I was out of my mind as they reminded me that the pregnancy was not only planned, but it was great news since they'd been trying for many months to have a baby. I would catch myself and try to backtrack by telling them I didn't mean it and their news was to be celebrated. Inside I was still in shock at why anybody would want to have a child. One part of me knew this was ridiculous thinking as I tried to reconcile this with myself. The other part of me couldn't let go of the fear of what a pregnancy would entail. I was relieved after my tubes were tied. I knew it was one of the best decisions I'd ever made and would never regret it.

About two weeks after my surgery, I had a rare Sunday afternoon free. I was wide awake and lying on my bed reading a book when three beings popped into my bedroom. I couldn't see their entire bodies, however, only from the middle of their chests and upward. The rest of their bodies didn't exist. All I could see was air until I got to their chests, and that's when they took form. There were two males and one female who looked like they could have been characters on Star Trek. They wore red and black uniforms with a triangular patch or pin attached to the upper left-hand side of their outfit. Their faces looked like what I can only describe as Egyptian with high cheekbones and almost black hair. The female had her hair cut to remind me of Cleopatra with heavy bangs and the rest at shoulder length. The males both had receding hairlines. Although they seemed similar, I could tell one male was older than the other just by the way their hairlines looked as the older males was receding much further back than the younger male. They appeared human but not quite; something was off.

Years later, under hypnosis, I discovered they were what I learned to call the Greys. The Greys are probably the most recognized group of ETs. They came into public consciousness on the cover of Whitley Strieber's book *Communion*. I learned that extraterrestrials can camouflage themselves and appear as humanoids or anything they choose so they aren't so frightening to humans. Why they thought appearing as very odd humans unannounced in someone's home was not frightening at all was beyond me.

These space beings didn't arrive through a door or window – they just popped in. As soon as they entered my room, I became paralyzed by something they did and couldn't move a muscle, even if my life depended on it. Surprisingly, I was shocked and confused but not scared. Maybe it was because everything was happening so fast; I didn't have time be frightened. After paralyzing me, they flipped me over on my stomach and lifted me up from behind by the waist so I was forced to be on my hands and knees. I was clothed, but this didn't seem to be an issue as they internally examined my reproductive organs. They were speaking telepathically and telling me how upset they were that I'd had the tubal ligation, which was interfering with their plans. I had no idea what they planned to do or why my choice to not have children was a problem.

During the exam, they also communicated telepathically with each other but I still understood what they were saying. They noticed that a tubal ligation simply obstructed the path of an egg going through the fallopian tubes; it didn't prevent me from releasing eggs. Once that was confirmed, they left as quickly as they appeared; and I was left in shock kneeling on all fours on my bed. The whole event, from them popping into my room to exiting, felt like it only lasted a couple of minutes.

After they left is when I panicked, trying to make sense of what had just happened. Had I fallen asleep and dreamt this? Had I been hallucinating? What the hell just happened!? As the visitation looped through my head repeatedly, I tried to find a rational explanation to what HAD just occurred. I knew I wasn't asleep. I knew I wasn't hallucinating. This felt so real, and the fact that I found myself on my hands and knees but was able to move again and not be paralyzed once they left was convincing enough. Over the next couple of days, I tried to find an explanation but could make no sense of any of it. I needed someone to talk to, but how could I tell anyone about this? Who would believe me? I barely believed it myself.

A few days after my extraterrestrial exam, a close friend and I were walking in her neighborhood one evening after work. We'd been friends for about 10 years and we both struggled with losing weight. Our walks were often cathartic as we could talk about almost everything it seemed. I decided to take a risk and told her about my uninvited company. Taking a deep breath, I told her my story. She was very kind and said she believed me, but I could tell she was struggling to comprehend what I was saying. At this point in our lives, she had no idea I was psychic as I was still quiet about that piece of my life. I could read the thoughts running through her head. I telepathically heard everything from "She's crazy, who else can I tell about this? Can the rest of our friends have her committed? Can we still be friends now that she's gone off the deep end?" I could tell by her thoughts that I could never bring this up again. Once again, I had to shut down a piece of me.

Staying quiet about this life changing experience was excruciating for me. I took one more risk and told another friend. Since I told her, she's never asked questions about what else has happened, which was my sign to say no more. However, she did introduce me to a co-worker of hers who also had an interest in UFOs. Tom and I hit it off immediately and he became my UFO go-to person. He was genuinely interested and intrigued in everything I shared with him, although he had no experience of his own.

I can't blame my friends for not necessarily believing me; I questioned myself every day. Who could believe this story?

Continuing my quest to find others to talk to about my experiences, I did some research and discovered Dr. Jack Kasher, who was the lead UFO investigator for Nebraska as well as a Physics and astronomy professor. I made the courageous move to call him and asked for an appointment. He was gracious enough to say yes. When the day and time for our appointment finally arrived, I was eager to tell my story to someone with impeccable credentials. I was nervous and scared that he would hear my story and tell me to go away, seek medical help, or worse, that I'd made it all up. To my amazement, he listened and paid attention to every word I said. He asked a few questions and then gave me his educated opinion. Someone finally believed me. I wanted to cry with relief. He also said this might not have been an isolated incident. At this time, I'd had only the memory of the one visit, so I struggled to wrap my head around the idea that multiple abductions were a possibility.

Dr. Kasher also told me there was a support group in town for other abductees. What? I had no clue abductions were a "thing", let alone there might be other people living in the same town as me with similar experiences. Tom, as my support person, attended the next support group meeting with me, mostly to hear other people's experiences of their own abductions. I was welcomed with open arms and asked to share my experiences. Hesitantly, I shared my story and felt that people were engaged in what I was saying. I was interrupted often by others, validating that similar exams had happened to them. The relief I felt brought tears to my eyes. I'd found my tribe.

I heard stories from others who had medically confirmed pregnancies that suddenly disappeared overnight. Most men in this group had memories of being taken aboard a craft and regularly having sperm taken from them. With every story I heard, I felt compassion for these people. They, too, were struggling to understand what was happening to them, comprehend things about life as we know it on Planet Earth and what it meant to be human, and question things beyond our planet. Alien abductions opened my mind to our not being alone. We have never been alone. Did aliens affect the lives of every human or just the few that remembered? Tom and I attended these meetings every month for about two years until business travel got in the way and the kind gentleman who hosted these meetings passed away.

A few months after my meeting with Dr. Kasher, MUFON (Mutual UFO Network) was hosting a symposium in Lincoln, Nebraska. How could it be that a year after I first learned of UFOs or abductions I was hearing of a UFO symposium just 45 minutes from my home?! Tom and I signed up to go for the weekend to listen to various speakers and learn more about the UFO community. One speaker was Linda Moulton Howe, an internationally known film maker and ufologist. At the end of her talk, she generously allowed time for questions from the audience, and I was lucky enough to be chosen to speak. I told her about my experience and subsequent exam and asked if she had an opinion or anything to add. She repeated almost verbatim what Dr. Kasher had told me months earlier; this probably wasn't an isolated incidence and that I'd most likely been contacted often but had remembered none of the other abductions. I walked away grateful for her opinion but shaken to the core that the one exam might not have been the only one. Would I eventually remember any other incidences? Could I handle remembering? I left, not sure if I was happy to have attended the symposium. It was fascinating to hear what the other speakers had to say. Other than Dr. Kasher, this was my first time listening to others who had made the study of UFOs part of their professions.

I left the symposium and, within a few days, headed to the library to check out books about UFOs, abductions, and all things related to ufology. I immersed myself in these books and wondered if there was any connection to the metaphysical information I'd studied for so long. My experience felt both physical and metaphysical. I was looking for definitions, parameters, and a way to label what I learned, to somehow make everything fit into a nice, neat box with logical explanations.

How was I to know that my introduction to ufology through symposiums and literature was just the beginning of what I would learn? What I was about to uncover made me question everything I knew about life on Earth. Through downloads of events flooding many of my waking hours for the next several years, I learned that the invasive medical exam I endured was one of dozens of involuntary takeovers of my body. I could only continue to move forward. I didn't have the option to say no.

"Two possibilities exist: either we are alone in the Universe or we are not. Both are equally terrifying."
Arthur C. Clarke, Science Fiction Writer

Hybrid Children

I was so grateful for my ET support group. Shortly after I joined, additional memories were downloaded into my consciousness. Aliens can manipulate you as they choose; so, when the downloads occurred, they often wouldn't be in chronological order, which only added to my confusion.

These downloads would happen during the day, right before I fell asleep or even during a business meeting. If they happened in public, I had to put on an expressionless face while these insane stories were being loaded into my brain. I was finally told, telepathically, that I was part of a breeding program, which was why that original group of ETs, the Greys, was so upset when I had my tubes tied. Later, images downloaded in my brain showed me on a craft where I was put on a gurney and prepped for another examination. I have no memory of leaving my home or being transported to a craft. My only memories, with this ET group, are of being on a craft – not being brought there or returning to my house, just being onboard.

The abductions always began the same way – the Grey ETs would enter my bedroom just as I was falling asleep. I couldn't see them, but I could feel them by a distinct energy change in the room. My heart would pound and sweat would pour out of me as I froze with fear. My next memory was of waking up in the morning, knowing something had occurred; but the details were fuzzy until the ETs downloaded the rest of what had happened. Many memories of being on crafts are fuzzy, but I've been able to recall them mostly in bits and pieces and finally through hypnosis. During several abductions, I was escorted down hallways dressed in what felt like a hospital gown and then placed on a gurney. While in these hallway excursions, I was shown large jars of fetuses in various stages of development. There was shelf after shelf, row after row, of these jars, sitting among other medical specimens and tools I don't clearly recall.

Once I was placed on a gurney, I could look around, moving just my eyes. It shocked me to see what appeared to be hundreds of other individuals on gurneys too. We were all in what I call the twilight sleep or alien paralysis. None of us could move at all. It's what I imagine it would be like for a stroke victim or someone with ALS – being of sound mind but no control over the body.

During one abduction, I remember seeing a gentleman right next to me on the neighboring gurney. He had bright red hair, which stuck in my mind as I have red hair too and made him different from the sea of others who'd also been abducted that night. Several months after that night, a gentleman walked into my place of business, and I froze. It was the same red-headed gentleman I'd seen on the gurney next to me that one night on a craft. I did talk with him privately and asked very odd questions in no way related to his visit. Fortunately, I didn't have to ask my questions for long as he immediately knew what I was alluding to and told me he was being abducted for years. While he had no memory of me next to him on a gurney that night, he had, like me, patchwork memories of various abductions.

In that abduction, gurneys were lined up, side by side, as far as I could see. It felt like the gurneys were attached to a conveyor belt as they moved effortlessly and in order to the main examining area, making a snake-like motion that mimicked the internal shape of the craft. As each of us got close to the "doctor" performing the examinations, there was a crew of helpers. One member of the crew would aid in preparations for the exam by lifting each person's legs into stirrups and exposing the male or female anatomy for the doctor to perform the exams.

The exams were brief but invasive to a degree that would coincide with the word rape or sexual assault. Neither the doctor nor crew members showed any emotion. There was no compassion or empathy, just robotic and perfunctory motions as they worked on person after person.

During the exams I was able to move only my eyes but saw shelves in the background of the examining room. These shelves were stocked with clear medical jars of human body parts and fetuses. I saw them, recognized what they were, and stared at them but without the emotion I would have if I had not been paralyzed and zombified by these space beings. After each exam I was escorted through another hallway, given my clothing, and transported back to my bed at home. There were many mornings I'd wake up with my head by the foot of the bed or spots of blood on my pillow. My genitals felt sensitive and violated, yet I always woke up alone.

The hallways leading to the rooms where my clothing was removed or put back on were very reminiscent of the metal detector I experienced in the Sioux Falls airport. No wonder I was filled with fear thinking about passing through that doorway to nowhere. I now know that it wasn't a doorway to nowhere; it was a doorway to hell.

By age 35, I was having severe issues with my female organs. One week I would feel pregnant, and the next I felt normal. There was frequent pain and severe bleeding during my menstrual cycle. The discomfort I felt didn't seem to stop or even reduce the number of exams I was subjected to by the ETs. Often, I'd feel like I hadn't been contacted in a few weeks, or even months, and just breathe a sigh of relief thinking maybe they were finished with me. Then a download would happen, and I was back on a gurney in a craft.

One particularly disturbing memory presented itself the morning immediately following an abduction. There was something different about this abduction. The real memory, and not a download, flooded my consciousness as I woke up and tried to get my bearings. I'd been brought on board a craft the previous night and was told that my daughter needed me. My daughter? For some reason, this was not shocking as I agreed to go onboard a craft and help. The Grey in charge that night told me that my daughter had too much human in her, was experiencing failure to thrive, and needed her mother. I didn't exactly know what that meant, but I heard and felt the urgency behind those messages.

I was brought into a very sterile-looking room and was told to sit down. This room, about the size of an average bathroom in a home, was white and, what appeared to be, stainless steel. There was nothing else in the clinical-feeling room except a chair. A few minutes later they brought in a little girl who, supposedly, was my daughter. She was just a tiny bit of a thing – so delicate and fragile looking. Her hair was pure white (as mine had been as a child) but sparse with a few strands pulled to the top of her head and tied with what appeared to be some kind of a ribbon. She looked so sick – pale and barely responsive. As I lifted her up and placed her on my lap, it felt as if she weighed almost nothing. She had the large black eyes of the Greys but, otherwise, no other common feature. The rest of her looked like a tiny, sick version of me.

Every maternal instinct I thought never existed in me suddenly ignited. I hugged her, kissed her, and told her I loved her. She clung to me like any sick child would cling to its mother. As she and I bonded and connected, I physically saw color come into her face; her skin developed a beautiful peaches-and-cream complexion, and a sparkle lit up her eyes. She looked more alive, more engaged, and finally healthy. Our time together seemed to last just a few minutes but could have been several hours, and I felt like I could never let her go. She was my daughter – my little girl. I was heartbroken knowing I eventually had to let her go.

When the Greys came back to collect her, I struggled to give her back to the non-emotional, vacant alien space beings now standing before me. However, as she jumped off my lap and scampered across the room to the ETs, I quickly realized that they were the only family she knew. They might not have had emotion towards her, but she certainly had emotion towards them. I had to let her go. I'd done my job; I helped save her – my child.

Earlier that night I must have negotiated a deal with the Greys before I was taken on the craft, but I have no recollection of doing so. As two of the Greys escorted my daughter out of the room, some of the others led me down a hallway to a set of double doors. Somewhere deep in my soul I knew that my little girl was not my only child. Evidently, my negotiations stated that I would help them, the Greys, with my daughter only if they would introduce me to my other children. Now, standing before the double doors, I was angry, nervous, and excited, waiting for the doors to be opened. When they finally did open, what appeared on the other side was a room the size of a small gymnasium with about 35 kids of varying ages, all staring at me. These were my other children? Their heights varied according to their age, but they looked to be taller than what we would call normal and were abnormally skinny, beyond lanky. They also seemed to have little, to no, bone structure. There was skeletal structure because something had to support their bodies, but there was nothing I could identify as humanlike, nor could I identify their gender. They all had the aliens' big black eyes and sparse strands of black hair. Unlike with my daughter, there was absolutely no recognition between any of us. I looked at them like the aliens they were, and they looked at me like a benign intruder. Now I understood why the beings told me my daughter had too much human in her. On Earth she would have been recognized as a human, albeit a strange looking one. The others had no human characteristics. It was easy to shut that door and move on. My next memory was waking up in my bed the next morning as the realization of what had just happened flooded my mind and heart. I was the mother to these hybrid children.

As the star beings were keeping secrets from me, I was keeping secrets from my friends and family. We each only exposed what we thought the others could handle. As the downloads continued to happen, believe it or not, scenarios from my past began to make sense. Up to this point, there had been so many mysteries in my life that parents, other family members, and friends couldn't explain. It felt like my life would always remain disjointed. But as memories flooded my brain, the puzzle pieces of my life formed a bigger picture. I spent hours journaling and meditating, connecting with my spirit guides, asking them questions, and looking for clarification from events in my past. My guides stepped up and gave me answers. Starting at the beginning, my spirit guides, via hypnosis, helped define and explain the physical symptoms I'd had since childhood that no doctor could help with but only explained away.

Let's Get Physical

I'd experienced so many odd physical symptoms growing up that defied explanation. Most were just written off as me being an odd child, especially when doctors could find no reason for my maladies. The physical symptoms, individually, would not cause alarm or worry in most people's lives, but putting them all together created a different story – a very different story only uncovered after months of hypnosis and listening to other abductees publicly speak about their experiences and physical ailments. I sat in shock listening to some of these speakers as I realized I had many of the same things happening but had no idea these random physical anomalies were connected to being an abductee.

My family owned a cabin on Lake Poinsett in northeast South Dakota where we would stay most weekends and for extended stays during the summer months when my siblings and I were out of school. We were lucky enough to own both a fishing boat and a speed boat, which I loved riding around on the lake. As much as I loved being in the water swimming, I especially loved the wind flying through my hair while in the speed boat but also the calm of the fishing boat where my sister and I would row around the lake until our arms could no longer move. Every time I'd get in a boat, however, I'd either throw up over the side of the boat or run inside the cabin to get sick in the bathroom. No one else in my family ever complained of motion sickness. No one could understand why this happened only to me and not, at least, to my twin sister.

In addition to motion sickness, the nosebleeds continued. A bath towel was usually draped around my neck to catch the blood. After what felt like forever, the bleeding would finally stop, and I could carry on. Several times as an adult, I would wake up in the morning with blood on my pillow. I'd feel my face, only to find dried blood in my ears or in my nose. By then I knew implants had been placed in my body. Often with animals, they are tranquilized then tagged – much like what happens with human abductions. I always assumed, as do most people, that the animals are unaware of what's happening to them since they've been tranquilized. Now I wonder if that's true. Whenever I watch a show on television where animals are being tagged I feel a deep sense of empathy. I can feel their confusion and fear in much the same way that I felt when being treated in that same non-emotional way and scientific way.

As a child, I loved school, especially music class. Music was something that always came naturally, and I couldn't wait for class and, particularly, our concerts throughout the year. During the concerts, we'd go to the gymnasium, stand on the stairs or bleachers, and perform for our families. As each class went on the stage, the next class would line up in the hallway, giddy with anticipation. Every concert, without fail, I would faint while standing in line. It would begin by me feeling overheated, then cold, then both simultaneously. My vision would fail, and down I'd go. One time I fainted on the stairs during the show. Unlike many of the other students with high anxiety about performing, I had none – I was excited to show off and perform for my mom and dad, who I knew would be in the audience. I later learned that being an empath, a person who feels and takes on other people's energies, is not only a trait of psychic mediums but also a trait of abductees. I was taking on the anxiety of the kids around me. Another trip to the doctor, and my parents were told it was my anxiety. I might have had other anxiety issues, but I knew I didn't have performance anxiety. I did suffer with stage fright as an adult, but back then as a child, how was I to explain that to my parents and doctors?

Around that same time, I also had severe jaw pain and was taken to a chiropractor. The chiropractor explained that I was clenching my jaw at night. He tried to adjust me, but nothing worked. They never questioned why I was clenching my jaw, only that it couldn't be fixed. As a child I had no conscious reason for clenching my jaw, but hypnosis later revealed that it was from the night terrors, wondering if that night was a night I would be taken.

I was also born with congenital knee issues and came into this world with misaligned tendons. This made my knees dislocate at various times during my childhood. Whenever my knees would dislocate, it was incredibly painful and caused swelling with fluid in the affected knee. The surgeon determined that I needed surgery on both knees, but surgery had to wait until I was at my full adult height. So, at ages 16 and 17, six months apart, I had two surgeries to operate on my knees. In preparation of the surgeries, blood typing was done where it was determined that I had blood type B+.

About eight years later when I was living in California, I had some minor outpatient surgery, so my blood was typed again. This time it came back as type A+. I asked the doctor if a person's blood type could change, and he just laughed at me and condescendingly said, "No, it couldn't." I told him about my knee surgeries where my blood type was determined to be B+ and asked if he could type my blood again. This time I asked if I could watch. The nurse brought out a rectangular white card with ovals printed on it, and each oval was labeled with all the existing blood types. To test for a blood type, a drop of a person's blood was dropped onto each oval on the white card; and a certain chemical was placed with an eyedropper on the card. The person's blood would coagulate in the appropriate oval that would, therefore, determine the blood type. To honor my request, the nurse drew fresh blood from my finger and placed a drop onto each oval. It easily coagulated right on the oval marked type A+. I was so confused but was assured by the nurse that the medical staff in South Dakota had made the initial mistake. I just nodded my head and left the office.

After I moved to Omaha, I became a blood donor. The first time I went to the Red Cross to donate, I was asked if I knew my blood type. I took a deep breath and told them I was A+. The nurse must have felt my uneasiness as she blood-typed me for this first donation. She came back with a quizzical look on her face as she told me that I wasn't A+ but instead B+. I nearly cried with frustration as I told the nurse about my changing blood type. Once again, I received a condescending look as she told me that it was impossible for blood types to change and I must have misunderstood all the previous doctors.

As I'd mentioned earlier, at about age 35 I had serious issues with my menstrual cycles. After a few years of increasing pain, my nurse practitioner referred me to a gynecologist. This new doctor and I tried everything to alleviate my pain but left surgery as a last resort. At the risk of too much information, there was one instance that sums up what I'd been going through for years. One rare day off in winter, I wanted to see a movie. I was having my period and wasn't sure if I could even leave the house due to the unpredictability of my periods, but I decided to risk it and loaded up on feminine hygiene products. About halfway through the movie, I felt the familiar wetness between my legs, so I left my seat to go to the ladies' room. When I was safely in the stall and able to pull down my pants, I noticed I'd bled through an extra absorbent tampon, a heavy-duty menstrual pad, my pants, and even my winter coat! I always carried extra women's paraphernalia in my purse, so I cleaned up the best I could and went back to finish watching the movie. As I approached my seat, I noticed that I'd bled onto the theater seat too. This happened in the space of an hour. Something was very wrong.

Finally, the day came when my doctor said we were out of options, and a full hysterectomy was scheduled for me. The doctor was originally confused as to why I was in so much discomfort since the tests previously performed only showed fibroid tumors in my uterus. After surgery, however, the doctor said she now understood why I was in so much pain. What she saw during surgery hadn't shown up on the test results. In addition to the fibroid tumors in my uterus, my ovaries were hemorrhaging and endometriosis was pressing against my spine. The doctor couldn't believe how much damage there was in my female organs. Well, I knew exactly why there was so much damage – years of use as an unwilling egg donor and my uterus being used as a petri dish had taken its toll. As I was being wheeled out of recovery and into my hospital room, I remember saying how good I felt. Physically, I did feel good; and emotionally, I knew I could never be used again as a lab rat. Little did I know how false that would be.

After a few years of being afraid to go to sleep, wondering if tonight would be "one of those nights", I'd had it. I was more angry than afraid. So, as I tossed and turned trying to fall asleep, I pounded my pillow and shouted into the dark bedroom, "What?! Were you born in a barn? Weren't you taught how to knock before you enter someone's home?!" I felt some minor justification with my declaration and promptly fell asleep.

A few nights later just as I was closing my eyes, I heard the distinct sound of knocking inside my head. Knock, knock, knock – the same sound as someone knocking on my door, asking permission to enter. I got the knocking I asked for, but it stopped there. Though no permission to enter was granted, I was gone to a craft somewhere. Months later, as I slept, I heard the now familiar knock, knock, knock in my head and knew I was about to be abducted. How could this be happening? I had no more female parts for the aliens to use and abuse. I next remembered being on a craft and on a gurney in the usual sea of beds. As the beds snaked their way around the room, one of the crew members did the usual prep of putting my legs in stirrups to prepare me for the upcoming exam. Part of me was confused, and part of me thought I had pulled one over on them. How surprised the doctor would be when he noticed my surgery! But none of that happened.

This time, I was with a different group of people going through a different exam. When it was my turn to be examined, my bed rounded the corner on the conveyor belt, and I saw that the doctor was using a different kind of tool. This tool was roughly the size of a small LED flashlight, about four inches long and one inch across. It also looked like a cord extended from the end of the tool and was attached to the wall somewhere in the background. The doctor placed this tool on my clitoris, and the electric shock almost sent me through the ceiling. This time it appeared they were testing orgasmic responses, and the tool produced an instant, although painful, orgasm. The next thing I knew, I was waking up in my own bed feeling so much pain between my legs to where I had difficulty walking to the bathroom. No, they weren't done with me yet.

Discovering the truth about my physical symptoms through hypnosis was in the front of my mind, but I didn't know who to go to – to whom I could trust. The only person in Omaha who I knew did hypnosis specialized in smoking cessation, weight loss, and stage fright. She wasn't the right person to help me since what I needed went way beyond what she could offer. I had to wait until the right person showed themself. Then I knew the time would be right for my investigation to begin.

Another physical anomaly was that I used to get migraine headaches. I would go from sitting at my desk at work, and within five minutes, I'd grab my wastepaper basket and vomit. I'd have to leave the office immediately, drive home, and climb into bed. The lights would have to be off and a pillow over my head to shut out any extraneous noise or light. The migraines typically lasted well into the night. The only way I knew the headache was ready to lessen was when I'd feel electric currents running up and down my spine. I'd be hidden under covers between bouts of nausea and trips to the bathroom waiting – waiting for the electric currents to be my sign that relief was just a few hours away. It felt like I was being re-wired, and my mind and body were being reconnected. The electric currents weren't painful; they were just not part of the normal function of my body.

When the pain had subsided enough for me to climb out of bed, I would try and make my way to the kitchen for some badly needed water. Sometimes I made it to the kitchen, and other times I had to race back to the bathroom and then back to bed.

The following day, when I was feeling better and could stand to be around light, I would make my way to the kitchen for hydration. As I made my way, lightbulbs would blow out. It usually began with the overhead light in the bedroom and would continue through the living room, dining room, and, finally, the kitchen. Not all, but at least one bulb in each room would blow out as I walked through. When LED lights were finally available and came with the advantage of lasting 7-8 years, I could hardly wait to get them so I could stop changing lightbulbs every few months. I spent a small fortune outfitting every light in my house with the new LED bulbs and felt I was prepared for the next migraine. These new bulbs did work, to a point. After the next migraine, I only blew out two lightbulbs, which had been in place approximately one to two months.

Once it got so bad, I left the lights off as I made my way to the kitchen for water, thinking that would be how to avoid the light conundrum. However, it didn't seem to matter. A lightbulb over the sink not only blew out but shattered, causing glass to fly all over the kitchen floor. The bulb was not even turned on, and it blew!

I needed to discover what was going on, and I hoped and prayed that the right person to help me would show up soon. Before the right hypnotist did show up for me, I had several more surprises in store. I had additional downloads, but this time, from a different group of ETs. What was going on? What the heck was happening?

Technology

I began receiving downloads of information from a
different group of ETs in the early 2000s. These
new downloads, which weren't scary but
intriguing, felt different than the physical exams
performed by the Greys. They began with me
sitting on a hilltop, in a craft. This craft was very
small, basically a three-seater about the size of a
round Volkswagen Beetle. I was being taught how
to fly a craft – a UFO! This new ET group
conducting these lessons did not treat me as a lab
rat but made me feel like one of them.

The lessons began with me learning how to take
off from a dirt road that resembled a short runway.
There were no markings, however, just a dirt road.
The hardest part was learning that mechanically
getting the craft off the ground was only part of the
process. The craft was mainly controlled by my
thoughts. I not only had to believe I could get the
craft off the ground but had to control my mind to
make it happen. The craft and I became one. It

would respond to whatever I was thinking and would go wherever my mind directed it to go.

I struggled to make me one with the craft. It was similar to that feeling I'd get when I was the passenger in a car and quickly come close to a stop sign. I was never sure whether the driver of the car saw the stop sign; and, not wanting to be critical of their driving, I'd attempt to help from the passenger side by pushing my foot through the floorboard in an empathetic effort to slow the car down. Learning how to get a craft off the ground with my mind gave me a similar sensation.

Learning to fly, on the other hand, was easy once I learned how to take off. In retrospect, it felt like taking off was the hardest part, harder than actually flying or eventually learning how to land. The lessons kept getting more and more complex as I was taught how to navigate between hills, then mountains, and finally between tall buildings. The most vivid recall was maneuvering between the skyscrapers of New York. When I was a buyer early in my career, I spent almost a week a month in New York and got to know the city well. Since I'd spent so much time there, I was very familiar with the cityscape and recognized it immediately. I didn't understand how we got to New York so quickly, in what felt like seconds, from Omaha, Nebraska.

What was amazing was the ability of this craft to swoop up and down and change directions on a dime and with no noise. The instructor and I always spoke telepathically, so noise wouldn't have been an issue anyway; but amazingly, this piece of flying machinery was so quiet.

After, I assume, passing the test of flying the small crafts, my next memory is of being on a huge craft. I have no idea how big the craft was, but the cockpit, where my memory led me, looked to be about the size of a large classroom. There was tiered seating with one huge clear windshield in the front used to see and for navigation. My instructor and I were towards the back; I was behind a long desk and seated in a swivel chair, and my instructor was standing to the side of the craft in front of, what appeared to be, a large bank of floor-to-ceiling computers.

My instructor was asking me to join him in front of the computers to practice programming. I laid my head down on the desk and acted like a petulant child, telling him I was tired and didn't want to do any more class work. I also reminded him that he knew I wasn't good at technology and didn't even like it, as anyone who knew me could attest to. Why was he making me do this stuff? He gave me the look parents around the world have given their kids when their patience is near the end. I knew it as the "mom look" or the "dad look." My instructor gave me the dad look, so I compliantly joined him at the bank of computers.

I don't know what came over me, but it was like someone turned on a light switch inside my head. I pushed buttons and did calculations like I'd been doing this my whole life (who knows, maybe I had been). As I was performing these button-pushing calculations, even I was shocked. How did I know how to do this?! And why was it so easy for me? My emotions turned from not wanting to do this to eventual boredom from doing this repetitively for so long.

Once that lesson was completed, I was told to go back to my chair. Soon a big movie-type screen appeared on one wall in the cockpit, and holographic images appeared. These images – natural disasters and horrendous fires filled with panicking people begging to be rescued – were horrible to see. These images were shown to me in the early 2000s many years before 9/11 and the horrible fires of 2018-19 in California. So, I knew this wasn't a memory or even a nightmare. I was then shown a group of people being affected by the fires and told I would be the one to save them. I asked if I could oversee saving my own family but was told there was someone else who would be handling my family and that I was to stick to helping the people assigned to me.

I then asked where this fire was located and how I was to help since I'd never seen a fire of that magnitude before, let alone fought one or saved a group of people. My instructor told me I would know what to do when the time came. I didn't need to concern myself with those details now but just needed to learn what he was teaching me so I would know what to do when the time came. It felt much like programming a computer with data that could only be accessed when someone turned the computer on and retrieved that data. Except, I was the computer. I was being programmed with information, which would only be useful when a switch was flipped and someone accessed the stored data in me. Evidently, this knowledge is stored or buried somewhere in my brain for future use.

In the research I've done since this new information was added to my downloads, I've learned that it is very common for abductees to be shown horrible disasters and told they'll know what to do when the time is right. This seems to be a common theme, but why, I don't know.

I had so many questions. When will the time be right? Have the disasters already happened, and I just don't know about it? Is it possible that I, and others like me, were all abducted and brought to the disaster areas to help – all without our conscious knowing? So many things have happened during my abductions that I'm convinced I've been allowed to remember only a fraction of what was done and what continues to happen. Will I ever know the entire truth?

After I spoke publicly about my experiences, very strange things happened. While I was in front of a group, I'd notice a look of shock on one or two faces, not the look of shock with what I was telling them but a very different kind of look. Twice, I had someone come up to me either during a break or after my talk was over and tell me they'd seen me before. Shockingly, they both said they saw strange lights in their backyards, and when they went out to investigate, they saw a craft sitting in their backyard! As they looked closer, they saw my face peering out from the windshield of the craft. I was driving the craft! These comments were unsolicited and came out of nowhere. I couldn't explain and didn't understand it either, but these people remembered and recognized me immediately.

When people share their stories like this, it does one of two things: it either validates what has happened or it means both of us are crazy. I pray it's a validation.

*"A purely psychological explanation is ruled out...
the discs show signs of intelligent guidance, by quasi-human
pilots...the authorities in possession of important information
should not hesitate to enlighten the public
as soon and as completely as possible."*
Dr. Carl Justav Jung, Psychiatrist

Hypnosis

After decades of compartmentalizing my life into disjointed puzzle pieces and keeping everything separate, I was tired. I was exhausted from keeping track of what I could say to some people and what I had to keep to myself. I feared being discovered, saying the wrong thing or having my worlds collide.

The compartments consisted of the corporate persona, the artist/musician/actress, the metaphysical person, the psychic/medium, and the UFO contactee. There were possibly five people who knew about all the puzzle pieces, but most people knew of a mere one or two of those very separate worlds.

The metaphysical piece continued to grow and flourish and was taking up more time in my life. For instance, I had an interest in becoming a Reiki practitioner for many years but did nothing to pursue a certification until an opportunity presented itself in 2013. I was paging through the flyer of the continuing education courses being offered through Metropolitan Community College in Omaha and noticed that a level I Reiki class was being offered the next day. The timing was perfect, but I'd missed the cut off date for enrollment. I called the instructor directly and asked if it was too late to join the class. Even though the class was full, she agreed to let me enroll. The next morning, I arrived at class with the exuberance of someone really wanting to learn and not with my usual snarky attitude. I somehow knew this class would have a breakthrough for me; I didn't know how I knew this, but I did.

The instructor walked in the room and my instant reaction was, "Oh, it's her!" My soul recognized her soul immediately, and I knew I'd come to the right class at the perfect time. While we were waiting for the rest of the students to arrive, the teacher talked about her last hypnosis session. I had no clue she was a hypnotist; I thought she was strictly a Reiki instructor. As she spoke about the hypnosis session, she didn't mention names but said that she and the client "went way out there". She explained that "way out there" meant they had gone beyond past lives and went to outer space, which included other planets. With that one statement, I knew I'd found the person to help me. If she was open to space travel, surely, she'd be open to ET experiences. I knew that the teacher that day, Gabriele Kohlieber, could help me make sense of my life – could help me fit the puzzle pieces together.

Knowing that I'd finally found the perfect person, I redirected my attention to the class. The first half of the class was devoted to the history and mechanics of Reiki. I knew little, if anything, about Reiki but was intrigued by the symbols implanted in me by the teacher. Students were also taught symbols to be used to activate the Reiki energy before a session with a client. It all felt very exotic and foreign. After a lunch break, we practiced on our fellow students.

That afternoon was one of the strangest I'd ever experienced. It was as if I had been doing Reiki all my life and that afternoon was merely a refresher. As foreign as the history of Reiki was, I instinctively knew what to do as I laid my hands on the lady assigned to practice with me. With each hand position, her body spoke. Her body told me about physical and emotional trauma she'd been through. There were even dead relatives popping in with additional messages. I kept my mouth shut during the session but knew I had to deliver these messages when my practice person was off the Reiki table. When her session was complete, I asked her to join me in the hallway for a private conversation. I delivered the messages, and every one of them was right on target. I don't know which one of us was more shocked: her for receiving these messages or me for delivering them to her. After that one class, I knew that I would have to continue the levels of certification and practiced such until eventually I reached Master level in 2018.

Days after that first class ended, I called Gabriele and booked a private hypnosis session. Gabriele was trained and certified in hypnosis by Dolores Cannon, a best-selling author and past-life regressionist and hypnotist. Dolores is still highly regarded as a trailblazer in hypnosis, and her career spanned almost 50 years until her passing in 2014. Gabriele had studied and learned from one of the best. Now Gabi was using that knowledge to help others, including me, in their personal quests to understand themselves.

As the day approached for my session with Gabi, I didn't quite know what to think. I'd been hypnotized before for a case of stage fright as an adult singer, but that was all. This new session with Gabi would expose a level of vulnerability I wasn't sure I was ready for. I was excited to finally learn the truth about my abductions but was frightened too. I was scared that, through hypnosis, I might be exposed and was so afraid that hypnosis would reveal that I'd made up everything, that I was a fraud regarding alien contact. On the other hand, I feared hypnosis would disclose that I hadn't made up anything, that all of it was true. I wasn't sure which was worse.

The day I arrived at Gabi's office, I was filled with mixed emotions. She and I talked for at least an hour as I tried to explain my abductions. She asked me what I needed to know – what I needed validated – and what questions I had regarding my alien contact. Together we compiled a list of questions, and then I was ready to begin. Some of those questions included, "Did I make up everything? Am I an alien? What is the purpose behind these abductions? When did the abductions begin?"

The induction finally began with Gabriele counting down and taking me deeper and deeper into a hypnotic state. When she was satisfied that I was in the appropriate state of hypnosis, she connected to my higher self and asked the prepared questions. I have no record of that first session, so all the information is coming from my memory. Although my memory can be faulty, like most people, the first few sessions were very clear.

Gabi asked me to go back to when the abductions began. Immediately, I went home. This home differed greatly from any home I'd ever lived in this lifetime. I found myself on a beautiful pink planet – a planet that consisted mostly of water. I remember the sheer joy in the simple act of dipping my toe in the water just to watch the ripples float away. This brought back memories of my love of water on the lake where my family had our cabin. Gabi asked where I was, and the only thing that came out of my mouth was the word home. I was home in the truest sense of the word. This is where I came from – my soul's first and only home. It now made sense when I reflected on the times of my life when I would walk alone at night, look at the stars, and beg to go home. I now knew where home was, what it looked like, and how it felt to be there again. I felt alive. I felt the peace and happiness I'd been chasing during my entire existence on Earth. The unconditional love felt true and honest even though there was no one there but me. I knew my fellow pink planet inhabitants were there somewhere; I just couldn't see them, but I could feel them and the love they were radiating towards me. Gabi asked what I looked like, and I explained that I looked like a small fairy-like creature. The only emotions I felt were love and joy. When I was asked to look around me and describe what I saw, I could barely find the words. The scene that unfolded in front of me was filled with other stars, planets, and moons. The colors were unlike anything I'd ever seen on Earth. The vibrancy and intensity of these colors were so bright, yet not painful to my eyes. In the distance I saw Planet Earth and immediately cried. The pain pouring forth from that planet was palpable. Earth was surrounded by a brown dust, and our beloved planet was breathing like someone who had been a lifelong smoker and was now choking, trying to find a last breath of air.

I could feel the pain, hurt, and violence pulsating from Earth. I continued to cry and questioned why we treat each other the way we do. My biggest questions were, "What was the purpose? What was the reasoning behind this kind of human behavior?" I didn't get answers that day nor have I since.

The answers I did get were that I had a multi-lifetime agreement with what many of us call the Greys. Some of these lifetimes were on Planet Earth; others were on various other planets. On several occasions I told the Greys to stop using me as a human lab rat, but each time they showed me a contract that included my signature. I'd resigned myself to honoring that contract as I am a person of my word. Now, in this first hypnosis session, my spirit guides told me this contract was false. It was only a ruse to keep me participating in their breeding program lifetime after lifetime. My guides also told me that because of Universal Law, I could rescind that contract at will.

My main goal in participating with aliens was to spend multiple lifetimes on many planets as a gatherer of information. The most recent incarnation was on Planet Earth, which is one of the most difficult planets in which to survive and thrive. In this lifetime I had agreed to be part of a breeding program besides being an information gatherer. It became very clear that the reason I'd had so many careers and lived so many places in this lifetime was to expose myself to different people, lifestyles, and careers and bring that information back to them – the ETs.

In this session, I was told that yes, I was an alien. But on Planet Earth, we were all aliens, seeded from somewhere else. That's why there are so many types of people on Earth. That is not the case on many of the other planets. I had the answer to my biggest question, wondering if I was indeed an alien. I was/am but not in the way I thought.

I was told that Earth is unique. It is one of the few planets where emotions other than love exist. With emotions such as hate, fear, jealousy, rage, lust, and greed, there was bound to be conflict. My job in this human incarnation and as a gatherer of information was to bring back to my home planet examples explaining why humans behave as they do and under what circumstances.

That first session ended with me not being sure whether I wanted to break my contract with the Greys. I hated being used as a lab rat in their breeding program, but I also understood the bigger picture – that my contact with aliens wasn't just about breeding. It was also about understanding human nature, figuring out why humans are the way they are, where they come from, and what information can be gathered and learned from human behavior. My mind was blown in that first session, and I absorbed all that I could handle. I needed to sit on the information, journal, meditate, and try to make sense of how all this new information could fit into my current human life.

My second session was a few months later. This time the major question I had was to discover whether I'd ever seen a UFO from the outside. My only memories were of being in a craft, not outside of one. I had distinct impressions of what the inside of various crafts look like but no memories of ever seeing the outside.

A little joke I used to play was when people would ask me if I believed in UFOs. This was always in casual conversation when there was nothing at stake, and I always answered that yes, I did believe in UFOs. The next invariable question was always, "Have you ever seen a UFO?" My answer was always, "Not from the outside." This answer was my way of gauging how open, attentive, or aware the other person was. Not once, in all the years this question was brought up did anyone catch what I'd said. I found that intriguing. Were people just not listening or did they not want to delve further into my response? I was always waiting for that one person to ask me to elaborate and ask what I meant when I said, "not from the outside."

In this second session, I wanted to discover whether the answer I always gave was correct. As Gabi started the induction, I could tell my soul was eager to begin. I went into hypnosis almost immediately. Things began in a very different way this time, however. Gabi directed me to go back to the very beginning, assuming I would go to the pink planet just like the time before. Neither of us expected what happened next. Behind my closed eyes all I saw was darkness. Nothingness. No light, no sound, no anything. I panicked as I told Gabi what I was or, rather, what I wasn't seeing. She directed me to move forward in time until I did see something. Then the most amazing thing happened. I witnessed what looked and felt like the big bang. It was an explosion that created billions of stars. Each of these stars was pure energy, representing a soul. There were still no planets, sun, or moon but, simply, billions of stars. I could tell I was one of those stars, and this was the beginning of my existence as energy before I was assigned the pink planet as home. Gabi asked me to look around to see if I recognized anything. My mind immediately looked to one side, and there she was – Gabi – as another star, another piece of energy. It's no wonder my soul recognized her soul that first day of Reiki training. We were "born" together.

After that amazing experience, Gabi and I continued to move forward with the hypnosis session by asking the other questions I wanted answers to, mainly if I had ever seen a UFO from the outside. The short answer is yes, I have seen hundreds of UFOs from the outside. The way this information was introduced, however, was when I was taken further ahead in time. How far ahead I have no idea, but I suddenly found myself in a wooded area where a UFO had landed. This craft was camouflaged by trees, bushes, and various grasses, but I could see a silver disk shadowed between the trees and went to investigate. This felt like it was most likely the first time I'd seen a craft as a human. I did not feel fear, but apprehension, as I approached the craft. As I cleared away the brush, the metallic color of the craft stood out. It was a brushed metal, like stainless steel, but not shiny.

As I walked around the craft investigating, I saw writing on the lower half of this disc-shaped craft. When Gabi asked what the writing said, I had no answer, simply because the writing was not in English. It was not in any language I'd ever seen written. What I saw was a series of symbols, which felt like they were used to identify this craft, similar to VIN numbers on cars. The symbols were large and black in color, which made them stand out against the metal of the rest of the craft.

As Gabi and I continued to move forward in this session, many more memories were validated. Yes, I was being taught to fly crafts, beginning with the smaller ones and then graduating to the large crafts. I was even shown that the largest of the crafts, which housed the smaller crafts, had open circles on the bottom of them. This was so smaller crafts, several at a time, could exit from the bottom of the larger "mother ship" and do their business, whatever their business was. I was shown that sometimes I was flying the larger crafts, and other times I was flying the smaller crafts. I didn't understand then why I was flying these different crafts at different times.

Subsequent hypnosis sessions with Gabi were shorter but revealed new information each time. One of the most profound things revealed was in my last session with Gabi. She asked my higher self what my spirit guides thought of my ET contact. The answer stunned me and yet made perfect sense.

We are all one. I've believed for decades that we all come from source or God or whatever you choose to call the creator and that we are here to express ourselves differently, according to lessons we want to learn or things we want to experience or accomplish. The answer my higher self gave was that when we believe we are all one, that means all of us – including ETs – not only humans. We all come from source or God but are expressing ourselves in different ways, according to our chosen purpose. This can be on Earth or any other place in the galaxy.

After my last session with Gabi, I tried a different hypnotist by the name of Amanda Olmscheid. Amanda is the co-owner of the Ascension Center, which instructs and certifies others in hypnosis. When she and I first met, she'd just received her certification. Together, we wanted to do some exploring. Personally, I wanted to get additional verification from a hypnotist with a different skill set than Gabi. You could call it "validation of my validations." Amanda wanted the experience of working with someone with ET abductions. It was a win/win.

The first session with Amanda not only validated everything I'd experienced in my sessions with Gabi but added additional information. I knew I was flying crafts but didn't know the reason. These new sessions revealed that, during my sleeping hours, I was living another version of my life – a parallel life, to be exact. Having a hard time wrapping my head around this new information was an understatement. Under hypnosis, however, everything made perfect sense. As each scene unfolded, I became more and more aware that we live in many dimensions simultaneously. I was told that my body needed rest, but my soul did not. My soul had work to do in other dimensions. My higher self chose for my conscious self to remember by showing my body resting comfortably at night but my soul inhabiting another form to act as a first responder on other planets. I was shown that I worked with a group of other first responders. We would fly crafts to other planets in distress and help them either evacuate their home planet or, if the planet was salvageable, help them manage their resources. Besides flying the craft, my job was to help with underwater life. Others on my team oversaw either vegetation, air pollution, species living on the planet, or animals, much like firefighters, police officers, and EMTs on Planet Earth go from place to place helping those who need them. This was our job, only on a galactic scale.

Being under hypnosis felt like my brain was divided into two parts. One part was the person interested in learning the truth and allowing all the scenarios to unfold; and the other part of my brain was the logical human who was amazed, scared, and suspicious of everything I was being shown. I was grateful the truth was finally being revealed but still questioned whether this version was really the truth, or if I was still being manipulated, and if I had the courage to share it with others.

"This was no ordinary UFO. Scores of people saw it was no illusion, no deception, no imagination."
Air Marshall Azim Daudpota, Pilot, Pakistan Air Force

Let the Healing Begin

I made a vow to myself in 2010, shortly after my mother passed away, that I would heal no matter what it looked like. I announced this to part of my family during an annual summer vacation. They looked at me with questioning faces and asked what I had to heal from. I didn't elaborate and just left well enough alone. They had no idea of my childhood trauma even though we were raised in the same house by the same parents. They knew I was different and difficult for my parents, but other than that, they had no idea.

I saw alternative healers for sessions in Reiki, Healing Touch, emotion code, and body code, among many others; but the real healing didn't begin until 2013 with that first hypnosis session. That's when the pieces of the puzzle formed an actual picture. My life made sense in the broader sense, rather than the smaller fragmented pieces I'd always seen. I began to realize that I wasn't a victim in my abductions – I was a willing participant. I could choose to stop what was happening or continue; it would always be my choice. I finally did choose to stop all ET contact. I rescinded any contract I had with them in my current life and any other of my lives affected.

When the abductions finally stopped, I suddenly felt lonely. Something in my soul felt empty. I felt like I lost a best friend. I spent most of my life scared to go to sleep at night, afraid of being taken and used like a science experiment. Why did I feel like something was missing when I'd decided to stop?

It was my choice whether to participate. I changed my mind and said yes to the technological contract but maintained my firm no with the Greys. Under hypnosis it became very clear that the Greys performing invasive exams was something I hated and no longer wanted to participate in. The technological group, however, gave me a sense of accomplishment and purpose. I was part of a bigger picture. I wasn't just participating in the human life I knew; I was participating on a scale that would not only help Earth but other planets and their inhabitants.

During this phase of healing, I continued attending the Reiki practice sessions. One night I went to practice, but no one showed up except the teacher, Gabriele Kohlieber, and me. She told me I would have to practice on her. I just laughed and told her that doing Reiki on her was like doing

Reiki on puppies and rainbows since she had energy on a similar level to both of those.

The minute I put my hands on her I knew something was wrong. I dutifully went through all the standard hand positions, but with every position, I felt sicker and sicker. About halfway through I told Gabi I would have to stop because I would faint or throw up. I found my way to the nearest chair, sat down, and grabbed a wastepaper basket. As I held the wastepaper basket in front of me in the event I vomited, I heard Gabi ask me if I wanted to know what was going on. I just gave her a sarcastic look that said, "Ah yeah, that would be nice." She told me that her mother had just passed away. The minute the words were out of her mouth, I knew what was going on – her mother was trying to connect with me, and I wasn't paying attention. I was so concerned about using the correct Reiki hand placements that I wasn't paying attention to the spirit of Gabi's mother. Gabi then said that if I didn't feel well, we could stop. I looked at her and said, "I feel fine." The thing is, I did feel fine. Once I discovered that it was her mother making me sick, the sickness left immediately. As I got up from the chair, I remember putting a symbolic stake in the ground and claimed my gift as a psychic medium. I knew that Gabi's need for closure with her mother was greater than my fear of being called a psycho instead of a psychic. I continued our Reiki session while also delivering messages from her mother.

I felt safe. Gabi was someone I trusted and believed in. I knew she wouldn't roll her eyes at me or judge. I just shrugged my shoulders and thought to myself that one more person knew I had psychic abilities, but at least it was a safe person.

A couple of days later, my phone rang. I nonchalantly answered the call when I heard a stranger's voice on the other end of the phone. A woman said she was a client of Gabi's and was told I was a psychic medium. She would like to book an appointment with me. What?! My hands shook as a plethora of thoughts ran through my head. What came out of my mouth was, "Certainly. I'd love to set a time to see you." Where did that come from? I took a few minutes to explain that I was relatively new at this. I didn't tell her that I'd been receiving messages my whole life but that I'd chosen to tell no one. The session was set for a few days later. I do remember putting that stake in the ground and now it was up to me to say yes to the universe. Yes, I was ready to be me – the real me – not some version of me I thought the world expected.

Word of mouth is how my business grew, and within a short amount of time, I had a legitimate business as a psychic medium. My business continued to grow along with my confidence. I learned to trust spirit and knew my job was to get out of the way and let spirit through. Within three years my full-time profession was that of a psychic medium, and, eventually, I added the title Reiki Master.

While I was building my business, I attended several metaphysical discussion groups. One of the smaller groups was run by Gabi in a classroom adjacent to her office. She invited me to speak about my ET experiences to her group. Was I ready for this? Once again, I said yes to the universe. Gabi was such a huge catalyst in my coming out of the psychic closet and understanding my ET abductions. I trusted her implicitly and had to say yes.

There were only about eight people who attended that next discussion group. I'd met several before during previous meetings. They had met me but had no idea about the ET experiences. I wasn't sure if this made me feel comfortable or nervous. This was my leap into trusting others with the vulnerability of my story. Would they laugh at me or show respect and compassion? I should have known that Gabi would only invite me into a situation where I would be welcomed. Once I told my story, I opened the discussion up to questions. People were interested and asked for clarification on many things I talked about. Yes, many questions stemmed from their own fear, but I understood as many of my own experiences with ETs came from fear. The people in this group were kind, compassionate, and above all, open minded. Their response gave me courage to tell more people and to finally verbalize that my main goal in coming out with my experiences was to form a support group. The support group I was introduced to over 20 years previously saved my sanity, and now it was my turn to pay it forward.

I met with the leaders of several of the other metaphysical discussion groups in Omaha and asked if I could be a guest speaker. Once I told them the topic of which I wanted to speak, without exception, I was given a resounding yes. Initially, I asked members of each group to please keep my identity private. I wasn't yet ready to go that public; for now it was enough that I was putting myself out there in private groups. Even though all the discussion groups were open to the public, most had many of the same people month after month, so exposure seemed somewhat limited.

Inevitably, my identity would eventually be revealed. On rare occasions strangers would approach me, saying they knew someone who had attended one of my talks and asked if they could have a private conversation with me. At first, I was upset that my name and face were out there, but, like many things in my life, I got used to it and realized people would not find out about my intended support group unless word got out.

In January 2018, I finally founded an ET support group that began with just a couple of members who had attended the metaphysical discussion groups and heard me speak. In the almost two years since, we now have increased to 24 members and are continuing to grow. It has been an interesting transition. Initially, conversation was strictly everyone's ET experiences. Since then and as we've all gotten to know each other better and become more familiar with each other's stories, the conversations have veered in many different directions. We always stick to topics of metaphysics but often theorize about the connection between ETs, metaphysics, and quantum physics and how they all fit together.

Shortly after the group formed, we added UFO watching to our list of fun things to do. A year earlier, I spent some time in Sedona and went on a UFO Vortex Tour. There I learned how to tell the difference between UFOs, planets, stars, and airplanes. I brought this information back to the group so we could continue to explore and educate ourselves in the UFO phenomenon. The feedback I've gotten from the group is that, just like me, they mostly needed someone to talk to in a safe environment. We were also lucky enough to have tremendous support from other metaphysical business owners who let us use space in their buildings for our meetings, all at no charge.

The final step in forming this group was to contact MUFON (Mutual UFO Network). When I was in contact with Dr. David Jacobs in 1994, he told me that a goal of his was to have a directory for people who have had UFO or abduction experiences and needed someone to talk to. The directory was to list at least one contact person per state.

When I contacted MUFON in 2018, I was told that no such directory existed yet, so I asked if I could be the contact person for Nebraska. There is a different directory, however, that exists. It lists the lead UFO field investigator for each state who does exactly that – investigates reported UFO sightings along with a team. That is very different than someone talking to and working with those who have been abducted. Both resources are badly needed in each state. After some research and investigation from MUFON, I was chosen to be the contact person for Nebraska.

I know abductions and ET contact vary from person to person as do each person's memories. I also know the healing process is different for each person. Although I am not a therapist, my goal is to offer support to those with ET contact and fragmented memories by way of introducing them to others with similar experiences. Just having a safe place to go can make all the difference. I hope that, as we near full disclosure, therapists skilled in this phenomenon are abundant and support groups are commonplace. My dream is that people are no longer afraid of the unknown happening to them in the night, and they have access to plethora of materials explaining what is happening to them, where to go for help, and who to talk to for comfort.

It dawned on me one day that the entertainment industry has it all wrong. Every movie, except for *E.T. the Extra-Terrestrial*, and every mainstream television show either makes fun of people who believe or uses scare tactics to have the public believing we could be under attack and that an invasion from ETs would mean certain death and destruction for the planet. We've all been brainwashed to fear the unknown and ridicule anyone who goes public with their experiences. We've also been taught to believe what our government has told us about UFOs not existing, yet almost half of the people in the United States believe in UFOs.

I do believe that some ET groups are here to help us as a people and as a planet, but I also believe other groups are not as benevolent. Much like people on Earth, there are the good guys and the bad guys. I'm grateful for newer shows, usually on cable stations, that are taking the risk and telling stories reportedly true about UFO sightings and abductions. They still have the element of fear, which is understandable, but some are telling another side to the story – that it's not all scary or silly or merely hallucinations coming from a few uneducated and delusional people.

We need more courageous people, such as former Presidents Jimmy Carter and Ronald Reagan, who have both claimed to have seen UFOs. Former US Representative from Ohio, Dennis Kucinich; former Governor of Arizona, Fife Symington; and astronauts Major Gordon Cooper, Donald Slayton, Major Robert White, Joseph Walker, Commander Eugene Cernan, Ed White, James McDivitt, James Lovell, Frank Borman, Neil Armstrong, Edwin (Buzz) Aldrin, Maurice Chatelain, and Scott Carpenter are all on record as having witnessed UFOs.

When sightings are reported on the news, in my opinion, the people who are witnesses to these events are made to appear ridiculous and uneducated. The consensus is that the public will believe nothing until someone respectable and educated, whose reputation cannot be disputed, comes forward. Can the reputations or education of presidents and astronauts be challenged? There have also been numerous pilots and celebrities who have offered their own sighting experiences.

As far as abductees, people can continue to laugh and ridicule. But would they laugh and ridicule someone who has been sexually assaulted? That's exactly what many abductions are – sexual assaults. I've worked with many assault survivors and several of them report that a "look" comes over their attacker. A look that makes them appear and act almost non-human. The general public sympathizes with assault victims and is horrified when attackers are described this way. What is the difference between non-human looking attacks and alien attacks? It is not the attack for both are uninvited and unwanted. It is the way the attack is perceived and how open-minded the public is. Can the public make the leap from a looking non-human attack to an alien attack? Maybe this is the next step in full disclosure. Hopefully, whomever is reading this will have empathy and enough of an open mind to consider the similarities before dismissing the person brave enough to reach out for understanding and help.

As more and more "believable" witnesses came forward, they paved the way for me to tell my own story. I am just a normal person –my education is questionable as I'm a college dropout, and, often in my younger years, I was not even respectable. But I am and always will be a truth teller – telling the truth to the best of my ability with the fragmented memories downloaded throughout the decades.

My journey of healing continues even though I have come such a long way. My puzzle pieces are now integrated; I have come home to myself, finally having the courage to tell my story to anyone interested and willing to listen. I am proud to be a psychic medium because I know I help people find closure and healing by helping them discover and claim their own power – and tell their own stories. I am finally excited to tell my experiences of alien abduction for the same reasons – to help others find peace and speak their own truth regarding their own experiences. I am constantly challenging my clients to go outside their comfort zone and try new things – to be brave. For me to legitimately ask that of my clients, I need to do the same for myself. I must be my authentic self to ask that of others – no matter the risk of public ridicule or disassociation from my friends and family. It's the chance I'm now willing to take. Are you?

If you've seen or experienced a UFO or been part of an abduction and want help, please contact www.mufon.com.

About the Author

Kristi is a Psychic Medium and Reiki Master who lives in Omaha, NE. Her purpose on the planet is to make contributions that leave this world a better place by empowering others to understand themselves better and their purpose for being here. She can be contacted on Facebook at Kristi Pederson Psychic Medium, or at www.kristipederson.com